Fossils Rock!

Calling all aliens!

Are you planning a holiday to planet Earth?

'Fossils Rock!'
Published by MAVERICK ARTS PUBLISHING LTD

Studio 11, City Business Centre, 6 Brighton Road,
Horsham, West Sussex, RH13 5BB, +44 (0)1403 256941
© Maverick Arts Publishing Limited August 2020

A CIP catalogue record for this book is available at the British Library.

ISBN 978-1-84886-696-6

www.maverickbooks.co.uk

Credits:
Finn & Zeek illustrations by Jake McDonald, Bright Illustration Agency
Cover: Guy Edwardes/Nature Picture Library, Jake McDonald/Bright.
Inside: Nature Picture Library: Juan Carlos Munoz (6-7, 10, 24-25, 27), Konstantin
Mikhailov (8, 22), John Cancalosi (9), Jose B. Ruiz (12), John Downer (13), Daniel
Heuclin (15), Jack Dykinga (16), Philippe Clement (17), Paul D Stewart (18), Guy
Edwardes (18), Juan Manuel Borrero (19), Nick Hawkins (20), Jim Clare (21), John
Cancalosi (23), Steven David Miller (23)

This book is rated as: Purple Band (Guided Reading)

Fossils Rock!

Contents

INCOMING MESSAGE

Dear Finn and Zeek,

I want to visit Earth soon and I would love to find out about the animals that lived millions of years ago. Is it true there used to be dinosaurs on the planet?

I hope you can help!

From,
Amba
(Planet Petri)

Introduction

Millions of years ago, Planet Earth looked very different. **Dinosaurs** of all shapes and sizes roamed the world. But there are no photographs of that time - there weren't even any humans!

So how do we know what dinosaurs looked like?

Most of our clues come from fossils. Fossils can show dinosaur bones, feathers, footprints and even poo!

7

So what exactly are fossils? Fossils are what is left of animals and plants that lived millions of years ago.

Dinosaur teeth

Dinosaur skull

Most fossils are formed in rock. They can tell us about all kinds of creatures, from tiny insects to the scariest dinosaurs!

Ancient insect!

This fossil of a dinosaur **skeleton** took millions of years to form.

Ornithomimus dinosaur

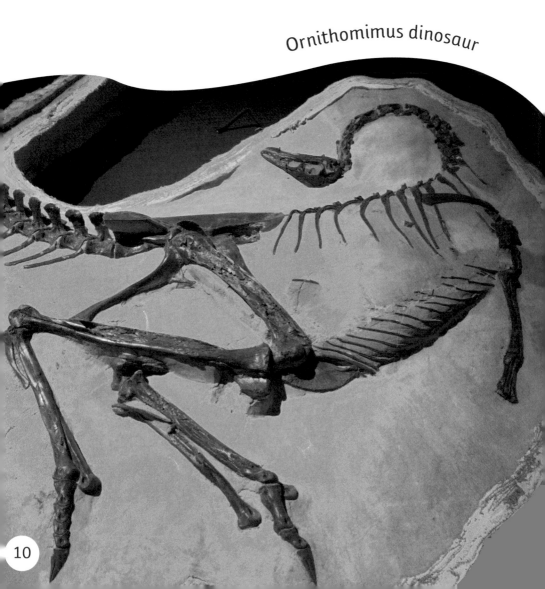

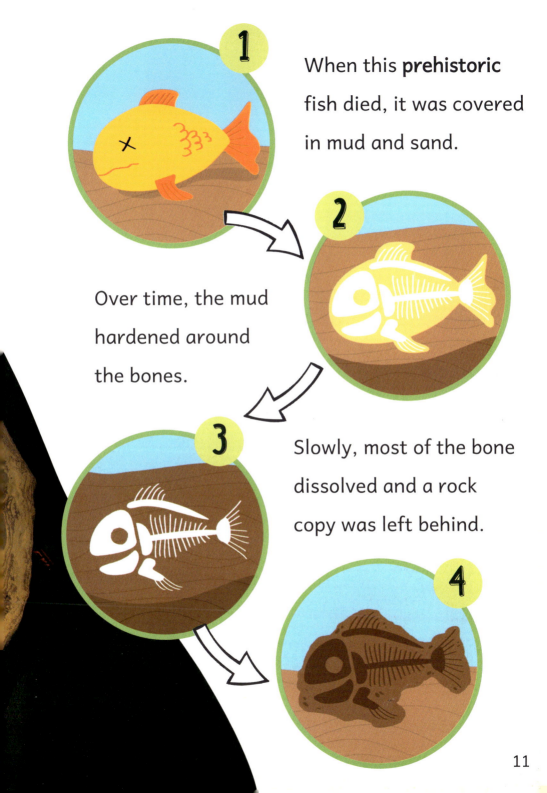

When this **prehistoric** fish died, it was covered in mud and sand.

Over time, the mud hardened around the bones.

Slowly, most of the bone dissolved and a rock copy was left behind.

11

Amber is a hard, see-through substance made of ancient **tree resin**.

The resin was so sticky that insects and other creatures sometimes got caught in it. As the resin hardened, the creature was **preserved** inside.

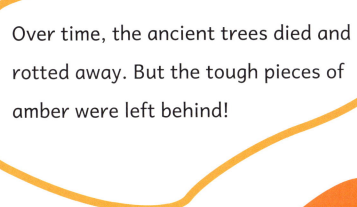

Over time, the ancient trees died and rotted away. But the tough pieces of amber were left behind!

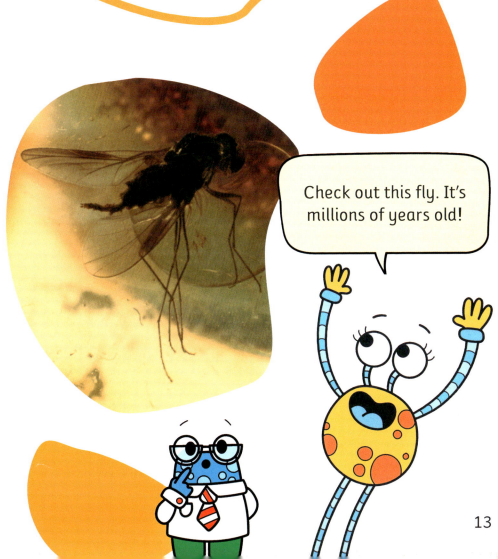

Check out this fly. It's millions of years old!

13

Ever wondered what a dinosaur had for breakfast? We can find out by looking at their poo!

Luckily poo fossils are so old they don't whiff!

A poo fossil is called a coprolite. All sorts of things have been found inside coprolites, such as tiny fish, leaves, seeds and little bones. This can show whether the poo belonged to a **carnivore** or a **herbivore**.

Walk This Way

Animal footprints can become fossils. These footprints, known as 'tracks', give clues to the weight and size of dinosaurs. They also show whether creatures walked on two legs or four and how many toes they had!

When dinosaurs stepped in mud or sand, their tracks usually just washed away. But sometimes these tracks were baked in the sun and went hard. Then, after millions of years, they turned into fossils.

Megalosaurus track

Where are fossils found? All over the world! Different types of fossils have been found in deserts, forests, oceans and mountains.

Planet Earth is always changing. Cliffs crumble, rocks **erode** and rivers dry up. Fossils gradually come closer to Earth's surface as these changes happen.

Wow! This desert was once a forest.

This is a fossilised tree!

Some fossils are uncovered by scientists who know the best places to look. Other fossils are discovered completely by accident!

All kinds of dinosaur fossils have been found across Europe. Two hundred years ago in England, a man called Gideon Mantell discovered the fossilised remains of a huge creature. He called the dinosaur *Iguanodon*.

Gideon Mantell

This curly fossil from Dorset, England, shows a sea creature called an ammonite.

Africa

Many scientists believe that the earliest dinosaurs were born on the African continent. It was also home to the *Spinosaurus*, which was as big as the *Tyrannosaurus rex* – or even bigger!

Fossilised starfish found in Morocco, northern Africa.

Ancient rocks in the USA and Canada have revealed some amazing fossils. This is where dinosaurs such as the *Stegosaurus* and *Brontosaurus* were first found.

Fossil site at Bay of Fundy, Canada.

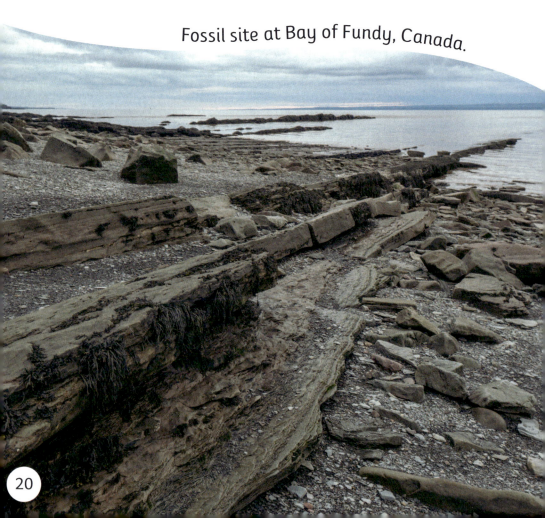

South America

In South America, fossils of **extinct** horses, elephants and whales have been discovered.

These are photos of a whale fossil found in Peru.

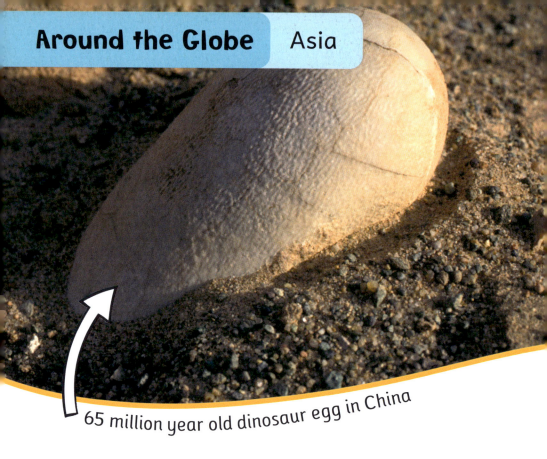

65 million year old dinosaur egg in China

More and more dinosaur fossils are being found across Asia. In 2019, a new type of dinosaur called a *Siamraptor* was discovered in Thailand. It lived more than 113 million years ago and had a fearsome set of shark-like teeth!

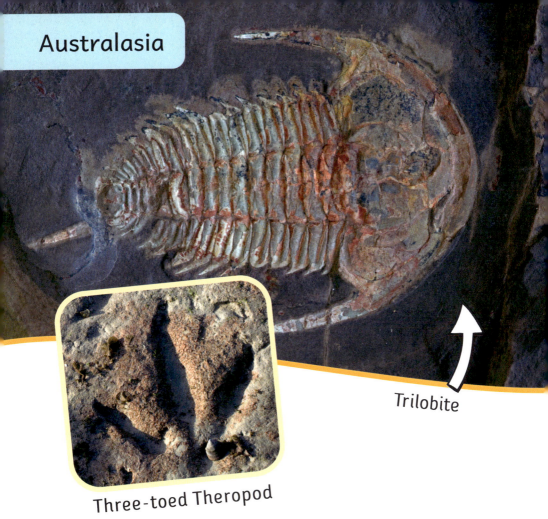

Trilobite

Three-toed Theropod

Collectors have found thousands of amazing fossils in Australia and New Zealand. These include early sea creatures called trilobites and the tracks of a three-toed Theropod.

Fossil Hunters

Scientists who study fossils are called palaeontologists (it's sounded out like this: *pal-ee-on-tol-o-jist*).

There have been many famous fossil hunters over the years. Mary Anning found new fossils in Dorset, England, nearly two hundred years ago. Another famous dinosaur detective is Dong Zhiming from China. He was born in 1937 and has discovered lots of new dinosaur species.

Anyone can hunt for fossils if you know the right places to look. There are still many to be found! What could be hiding beneath your feet?

MESSAGE SENT

Dear Amba,

It's true! There were dinosaurs on Earth millions of years ago. Fossils are like pieces of a giant puzzle scattered all over planet Earth.

Maybe you will find more clues when you visit!

From,
Finn and Zeek x

This is the skeleton of a *Maiasaurus*, a type of duck-billed dinosaur. Quack!

1. What is a coprolite?

a) A tooth fossil

b) A poo fossil

c) A toenail fossil

2. What colour is amber?

a) Purple

b) Black

c) Orange

3. What is this fossil creature called?

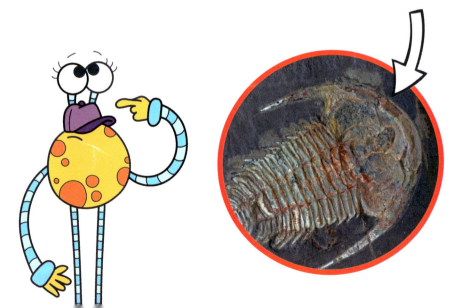

4. A new type of dinosaur called *Siamraptor* was discovered in...
a) Thailand, Asia
b) New York, North America
c) Kenya, Africa

5. What was the name of the famous fossil hunter in Dorset, England?
a) Ann Marry
b) Megan Ant
c) Mary Anning

6. An ammonite was a type of...
a) Mammal
b) Sea creature
c) Plant

Turn over for answers

Index/Glossary

Carnivore pg 14

An animal that eats mostly meat.

Dinosaurs pg 6-10, 14-15, 18-19, 20, 22, 24

These are creatures that lived on land millions of years ago. The name comes from two Greek words meaning 'terrible lizard.' Fossil remains of over 700 different types of dinosaurs have been found across the world.

Erode pg 16

This is when a natural surface like rock or soil is slowly rubbed away by water or wind. Fossils sometimes appear when a surface erodes, but this can take millions of years!

Extinct pg 21

When an animal or plant can no longer survive on Earth, it disappears completely and becomes extinct. Scientists believe that dinosaurs became extinct about 65 milion years ago.

Herbivore pg 14

An animal that eats only plants, such as fruit, grass and vegetables.

Prehistoric pg 11

The time before history was written down. The prehistoric age ended about 4,000 years ago.

Preserved pg 12

When something is kept without being damaged or destroyed.

Skeleton pg 10

A skeleton is a collection of bones that supports an animal's body.

Tree resin   pg 12

A thick, sticky liquid that oozes from the bark of a tree. Resin helps to heal any damage to the tree trunk or branches - it is like a bandage over the bark. Tree resin can harden over time to become amber.

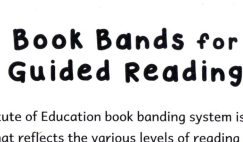

Book Bands for Guided Reading

The Institute of Education book banding system is a scale of colours that reflects the various levels of reading difficulty. The bands are assigned by taking into account the content, the language style, the layout and phonics. Word, phrase and sentence level work is also taken into consideration.

Maverick Early Readers are a bright, attractive range of books covering the pink to white bands. All of these books have been book banded for guided reading to the industry standard and edited by a leading educational consultant.

Pink

Red

Yellow

Blue

Green

Orange

Turquoise

Purple

Gold

White

Fiction

Non-fiction

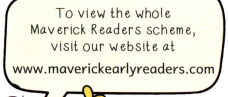

To view the whole Maverick Readers scheme, visit our website at

www.maverickearlyreaders.com

Or scan the QR code above to view our scheme instantly!

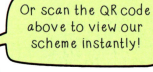